This is Darren
and his mother.
Sometimes he calls
her 'Mummy' but
mostly just 'Mum'.

Sally grew inside her mum's tummy for nine months before she was born.

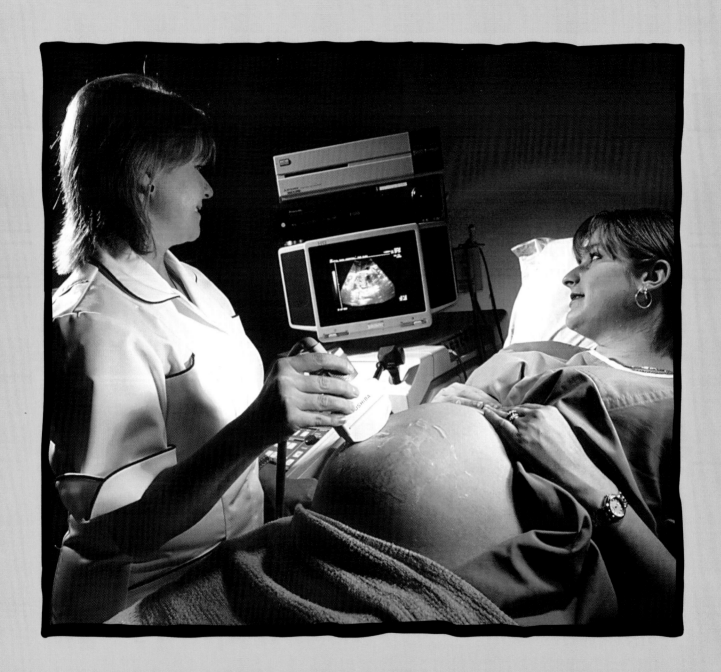

Jake was adopted when he was six weeks old. His mum has loved him ever since.

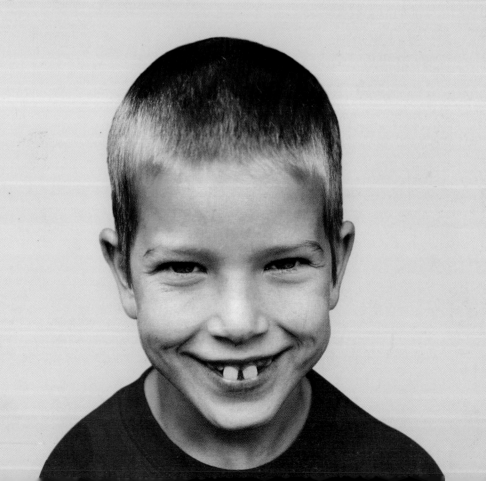

Lizzie has two mums. Her step-mum lives with her dad and Lizzie stays with them at weekends.

# David's mum
# works in a hospital.

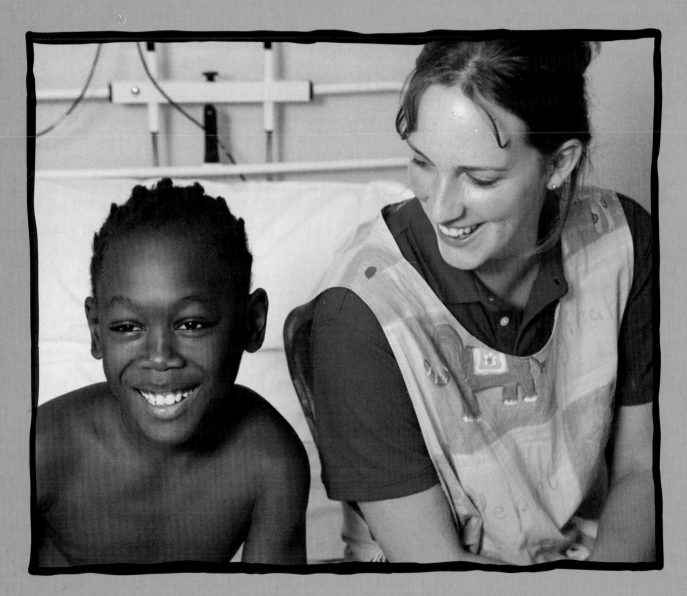

Chai's mum
works in an office.

Susan's mum
is a teacher.

Jason's mum is at home,
looking after his baby
brother – and Jason!

Polly's parents take it in turns to collect her from school.

Her mum comes on Mondays, Wednesdays and Fridays.

Mary-Jo likes going
shopping with her mum.

Ahmed likes it when he and his mum play in the park.

Paula's mum cooks tea for all the family when she gets home from work.

Ben and Emma's mum
tucks them up at night.
She tells good stories.

This is Maria
with her mum
and her mum's
mum – Maria's
granny!

# What's your mum like?

# Family words

Here are some words people use when talking about their mum or family.

Names for Mum:
**Mother, Mummy, Mum, Ma, parent.**

Names for Dad:
**Father, Daddy, Dad, Pa, parent.**

Names of other relatives:
**Son, Daughter; Brother, Sister;
Grandchildren; Grandparents; Grandmother,
Granny, Grandma; Grandfather, Grandad,
Grandpa; Uncle; Aunt, Auntie; Nephew, Niece.**

If we put the word 'Step' in front of a relative's name, it means that we are related to them by marriage but not by birth.

When people are adopted, they become part of a family by law, although they were not born into that family.

# A family tree

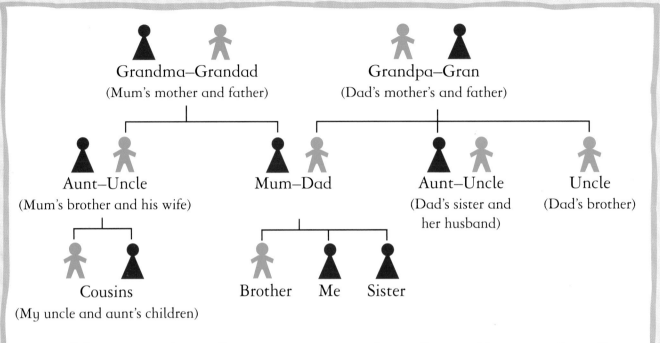

Grandma–Grandad
(Mum's mother and father)

Grandpa–Gran
(Dad's mother's and father)

Aunt–Uncle
(Mum's brother and his wife)

Mum–Dad

Aunt–Uncle
(Dad's sister and her husband)

Uncle
(Dad's brother)

Cousins
(My uncle and aunt's children)

Brother    Me    Sister

You can show how you are related to all your family
on a plan like this one. It is called a family tree.
Every family tree is different. Try drawing your own.

Published in 2008 by Franklin Watts,
338 Euston Road, London NW1 3BH

Franklin Watts Australia
Level 17/207 Kent Street, Sydney NSW 2000

Copyright © Franklin Watts 2003

Series editor: Rachel Cooke
Art director: Jonathan Hair
Design: Andrew Crowson

A CIP catalogue record for this book
is available from the British Library.

ISBN 978 0 7496 8105 0

Printed in Hong Kong/China

Acknowledgements:
Peter Beck/Corbis: 11. Bruce Berman/Corbis: front
cover centre below. www.johnbirdsall.co.uk: front
cover centre top, 6, 7, 10, 12, 18. Deep Light
Productions/ Science Photo Library: 5. Dex Images
Inc/Corbis: 20-21. George Disario/Corbis: 2. Carlos
Goldin/Corbis: front cover centre above. Don
Mason/Corbis: 1, 13. Brian Mitchell/Photofusion:
15, 19. Jose Luis Pelaez/Corbis: front cover bottom.
Ulrike Press/Format: 17. George Shelley/Corbis:
front cover main, 22. Ariel Skelley/Corbis: front
cover centre, 8. Christa Stadtler/ Photofusion: 16.

Whilst every attempt has been made to clear copyright should there be any inadvertent omission
please apply in the first instance to the publisher
regarding rectification.

Franklin Watts is a division of Hachette Children's
Books, an Hachette Livre UK company.
www.hachette.livre.co.uk

Please note that some of the pictures in this book
have been posed by models.